What My Hand Say

What My Hand Say

Poems

Glenis Redmond

Press 53
Winston-Salem

Press 53, LLC
PO Box 30314
Winston-Salem, NC 27130

First Edition

Copyright © 2016 by Glenis Redmond

Cover design by Kevin Morgan Watson

Cover art, "Behold His Face," Copyright © 2000
by April Wilson Harrison, used by permission of the artist.

Author photo by Mary A. Brown

Printed on acid-free paper
ISBN 978-1-941209-45-5

Dedicated to my great grandfather Will Rogers

and my grandson, Julian Josiah

ACKNOWLEDGMENTS

The author wishes to thank the editors of the following publications in which these poems previously appeared:

Appalachian Heritage: "Footnotes," and "Marked by Fire"

Appalachian Journal: "Churn"

Cave Canem 2010-12 Anthology: "Cotton and Cane"

Comstock Review: Anniversary Edition: "Dizzy"

The Cortland Review: "It's Complicated"

Flycatcher Journal: "Chair"

KAKALAK: A Journal of Carolina Poetry and Art: "I'm Fly"

Meridians: feminism, race, transnationalism: "Fried" (as "My Father's Ways)," "Benediction"

Nazim Hikmet Poetry Chapbook: "On the Way to Grandma's Funeral," "What My Hand Say," and "Crystal Clear"

North Carolina Literary Review: "Blue Bottles"

Orion Magazine: "Nature Lesson," "We Not That Carefree," "Genealogy"

Qarrtsiluni: "Bruised"

Red Rock Review: "Field Cotton," and "Praise Dave"

Silver Birch Press: "The Tao of the Black Plastic Comb"

Tidal Basin Review: "We Swag before Doo Rags"

Toe Good Poetry: "Apologia to My Double Ds"

Tongues of the Ocean: "Stomach Trouble"

When Women Waken: "Tilted Bowl," and "Ritual"

WNC Woman Magazine: "Story" (as "Stories")

Contents

Pull

Those who sow in tears shall reap with joyful shouting.

Psalms 126: 5

Pick

take hold of and remove (a flower, fruit, or vegetable) from where it is growing

Stories

Some hate the stories I tell,
Say, *Don't go back,*
as if my mouth
is connected to their hearts.

My head bowed
eyes intent on the stitch,
not busy with blame—
I work the pieces,

render the trade I learned
at my mama's & my grandmama's hands.
We call it *making somethin out of nothin.*

These stories are useful things,
stitches I follow.
They guide me clear,
and help me stand.

Rachel Cunningham

May the works I've done speak for me.
— Keith Johnson & The Spiritual Voices

Great-Grandma presses her memory down,
Every thang lived, chile, ain't written.
Every time I say, *grandma speak,*
From the beyond, she says, Listen:

My womb flowered 16 times.
Each and every honey-colored footstep I took
fell hard on the ground.
I picked over my weight in cotton:
as much as any a grown man.

Follow my life, it will lead you
down to where my bones are buried
unknown in the soil of Waterloo.
Stand at the edge of my life that blank slate,
with no recording not even a tombstone.
Nothing that marks that I ever lived on this land.
The same land I picked all my days.
Find me and my story.
Fill my empty slate,
but let my works speak.

Field Cotton

We stand not on the edge, but in the middle of the field
in between this white blaze that God made.

Our minds not fixed on the North Star, but grounded
to the weight in our bones as we pick, prick and bleed,

drag from what seems like Genesis to Revelation.
We are bred and wed to this cotton spur hold.

We sing hymns like *Steal Away,* but we know these songs
be the only thing we'll ever know of wings.

How can something so comely turn so ugly?
When greed wraps its hand around the land,

cotton becomes a field of lies acting like the truth.
This cotton crop got too many mouths,

works us *from can't see to can't to see,*
with two cotton sacks strapped across our backs,

we forget how we once dreamed
to be turned up like sunflowers in praise,

or how we once prayed to be woven to a greater whole
linked by the right hand of fellowship singing,

How do you do, sir? How do you do, sir?

We know nuthin 'bout freedom in this heat.
We got a blind eye and a deaf ear to everything,

'cept to what's at hand. Cotton—running in straight rows
the only train we was ever meant to ride.

Cotton Goods

You gonna tell the bad about cotton,
you might as well spell out the good right long side it.
At that task I have trouble.
Wonder why mama don't,
but picking 250 lbs. a cotton a day
she's got Field Creds.
She's either a saint or seamstress
working in Ware Place at Model Coats
for $1.25 per hour on 12-hour shifts
embroidering on cotton housecoats.

When I was 12, I use to ask her, *you tired mama?*
She'd just sorta of smile and say, *it beats picking cotton.*
Five feet even, she was the tallest
that she ever was in those words.
I looked up to her and how she'd measure
yards from chin to arms length.

Now,
I wonder how she manages
to look past plantations.
Maybe cotton in itself is quite beautiful,
but our broken-back lineage blocks my sight.
Those white clouds always spell misery,
but she's talking about putting
clothes on our backs.

In the fabric store, I watch her taking in
the multi-colored bolts. Everyone
must have looked like possibility, but
I was just a kid and I was bored,
but what did I know of how far she'd come
from the cotton sack dresses that she wore
to stand in this store and talk shop?

Her knowledge seemed encoded:
knowing 45 inches from 60 inches width by sight.
Or, even what the nap of fabric meant.

After the long and laborious fabric choosing
then speculating over notions.
This process in my young mind seemed endless;
I thought just stab me with a needle in the eye.

Her no way out of a way
had escaped my youthful ignorance.
The many emotional miles it took
for her to have options: buttons, zippers and bobbins.
I know now that she was taking me to school—
giving me a lesson of how to focus.
Train my eye—not on how we fall apart,
but how we learned to piece by piece
stitch ourselves back to together.

Nature Lesson

1947.
at age eleven
my mama learned
how a rope turns
into more than just a rope
looped around a branch
where a tree becomes
more than just a tree
where memory twists
around more than just the mind
like Willie Earle's neck
and my mama's young heart.
In Greenville, South Carolina,
Mama sees how memory hangs
on
each
and
every
limb.

Bale

When you gotta go. You leave. Take fear and every gift God gave you.
Shove it in half the space of a man. Tuck yourself whole self
amongst those same white blooms that you picked
underneath South Carolina sun. Ride the grain of this dark bloom,
in hopes to come out on the other side a larger man,
walking with freedom, but for now, breathe cotton dust,
eat mostly the same. Swamp water would beat back
your six-week thirst in this box that held you headed for Boston.
Drill holes with the gimlet that you are packin. Peep the stars.
Dream about a place where you don't have to worry
whether bale is noun that buries you soft in a white cushy grave
or verb that you ride to become the master of your own world.

Summon

Call him. Raise him up out the seat.
Free of window shield.
Free of neck break.

Give your mama something more
than the bits and pieces
that she has patched together.

Resurrect the man,
the mahogany frame.
Give her a chance
to stand by her dad—
hold his hand
lifeline to lifeline extending
beyond the four years
that she knew him.

Stoke and stir
turn and turn
until the mist
gives up the memory,
more than ghost
more than the echo
that fills your bones.

Until you see him: Will Todd,
a gentle apparition.
Hear the quiet wind of his voice,
the hum of his words
as he tells you how he followed the crops
season to season without fear.
Learn how he walked
upon the red clay with a soft foot.

Rewind. Stop just before
the 1939 Laurens County State Fair.
Pull back his hand pushed by gravity

to purchase the winning ticket
of the black sleek Chevrolet.

Cut short the joyride
and the fast road into fate
smooth out the hard curve,
the mean turn. Leave his life
to more than chance teetering
on a fickle raffle with the highest stakes.

Raise him up out the seat
free of window shield
free of neck break.
Stoke and stir,
pull and prod.
Bring him back
conjured and whole.

On the Way to Grandma's Funeral

The woods are dangerous.
— Little Red Riding Hood

You set a South Carolina record for footprints.
One hundred and nine years is a long time

for anyone to walk down a road.
My memory of you is as soft as the calico

housedresses that you wore.
The day you left, a quiet in us got up

and went too. We felt the terror rip through us
just like those large X'd flags waved

their heated tongues on the way to Waterloo
to bury you. They said nothing.

They said everything. How you meted your days
in Upstate heat. Coaxed flowers

like your head, *unbowed* and *unbossed.*
Your red Canna Lilies flaming like your spirit,

the tallest of tall; our limousine, a submarine,
sailed along holding your only living child:

mama and her five. We did not talk of the four flags
that we floated by, but we counted them all.

I don't even know how the talk started
of our top three desserts. Willie says:

1) sweet potato pie, 2) sweet potato pie,
3) that would be more sweet potato pie.

We rode on this laughter that you would have loved,
joined in with *Hush yo mouth, chile.*

You'd be proud of how we turned our heads,
away from hate: fixed our minds on sweet thangs

that stirred you 39,872 mornings
to lift from your bed, to rise.

Plow

turn up the earth of (an area of land) with a plow, especially before sowing

Elegba

Grandma can't be defined, I decided,
or put on a shelf, where I have tried to place her
alongside her well-worn King James,
next to her pastel Sunday-go-to-meeting hats.
I've always seen her with a Hopewell Baptist Church halo,
but grandma had this way of not being hemmed in
even by the gospel she upheld.
After she died I learned how she wore
a red flapper dress and shimmied to Fats Waller
as he sang through the gramophone.
Grandma always had something up her sleeve.
First time I heard her sling a slur I was counter-spun
at the NHC nursing home in Clinton.
Grandma was mumbling to who knows who—
probably somebody who had already crossed over,
perhaps a beau from long past ,
a vision in the room she alone could see:
Hmmm? What?
I ain't nigga 'nough for ya?
Her low growl, a flirt, then a turn,
a deliberate look into my eyes
as she spun this jazz.
Steps as if to say,
watch and *keep up,*
dance with me between worlds.

What My Hand Say

For great-grandpa, Will Rogers,
born in the 1800s

My hand say, *Pick, plow, push and pull,*
'cause it learned to curl itself around every tool
of work. The muscles say, *bend yourself like the sky,*
coil blue around both sun and moon.

Listen, my back be lit by both. My hand
got its own eyes and can pick a field of cotton
in its sleep. Don't mind the rough bumps—
the callused touch. I work this ground

like it was my religion and my hands
never stop praying. Some folk got a green thumb,
look at my crop and you'll testify my whole hand
be covered. I can make dead wood grow.

I listen to my hand, it say, *Work.*
My hand got its own speech. It don't stutter,
it say, *Work, Will.* Though it comes to mostly nothin,
this nothin is what I be working for.

Come harvest time I drive the horse
and buggy to town. Settle up.
This is where my hand loses its mind,
refuses to speak.

Dumb-struck like the white writing page.
The same hand fluent on the land,
don't have a thang to say around a pen.
The same fingers that can outwork any man

wilts. What if I could turn my letters
like I turn the soil? What if I could
make more than my mark, a wavery X
that's supposed to speak for me?

Praise Dave

Enslaved potter-poet
Edgefield, SC

First time I see a jar rise up,
I be midwifed into life.

Understood how these pots and I be kin
—dismissed to what's under foot.

I learned to turn and turn—
people the world with pots.

I pour my need into the knead
until forty thousand around me crowd,

but everything I love, I lose
so I want what I mold to hold.

Even my empty pots
be full. One say:

I wonder where is all my relations
Friendship to all—and every nation.

There are lanterns in my words—
every story got another story.

Some call me Dave the Slave, if that's all they got,
I say leave the rhymes to me.

When people look at me, a slave be
the first excuse they use not to see me.

I say praise me. It won't fall on deaf ears.
I catch praise like most people catch naps.

I am a 6-foot vessel of anything, but ordinary
a one of a kind with a Carolina shine.

I stepped out of the rows of cotton
to master the potter's wheel.

I take the wind out of can't.
With my mark, I make a mark.

I sign my name Dave.
I don't write slave.

See if my pots and me put a spin on history.
See if we   hold   hold   hold.

Dizzy

For John Birke "Dizzy" Gillespie,
born in Cheraw, South Carolina

Cheraw sounds like an Indian curse
or a blessing, depending
on how you let it leave your lips;
either way you ride this word
following music's bent lead

right out

of that shot gun shack existence that bore you.
Then, climbed North 'til it made you—Dizzy.
What did they know of the forces
of air that you chased—

dreams & eddies

held in the swells of your cheeks?
What did they know of the Slave Root
and the Choctaw Bone and the Dark Waters
that ran through you?

The blood rush

in your father's drunk fist,
that smashed the music into you
—the hammer falling in a small town

how it haunts

your memory with a blow.
You playing the horn, your heart heaving
in each note reaching your parents
in the colored row?

This moment speaks,

says leave this wind ache
to catch a better breeze.
Ride another wing than the one
feathered by Jim Crow.

Claim the current

you were always meant to ride,
where nobody can shaft
your breeze or steal the destiny
held in your lungs.

Blow the balloons

of your cheeks beyond belief.
Play like a divinity,
so we can sail on your song
across all divides.

I'm Fly

For Clayton "Peg Leg" Bates

Some people got two good feet
and still don't know what to do.
My smoothness makes the argument
for just one. My other leg be long gone,
sacrificed to the cotton gin god.

They pinned my mangled mess down
to the kitchen table. Made me suffer more
under the hand of an unsterilized knife
with only a cotton bit to bear the pain.

I got up and spit out that terrible taste
of Jim Crow and pity. Spun my mama's guilt
and worry into a dance that twists past
the neighbors' prayer, gossip and stares
of how he gonna make do with just one leg?

I strap on my dreams with tux, tails and flair.
Turn can't into can without losing time
not even in my mind. This Fountain Inn son
done good, I knock beats on wood.
I'm a worldwide showstopper all right.

Shout rings around all those two-footers.
I'm the master of my own fate,
when the world cut me at the thigh
I don't shuffle off in misery,
I get up on my one good leg and fly.

Churn

Mama's house
holds history high
on a shelf where a Carolina
clay pot sits, though I never churned,
I yearned to know how my family got over,
made our way through working
the land: the days that flowed
like sweet milk, turned golden
soft and easy—mounds of butter.
Then, the rough days too, without
cream, sour days, harder to swallow,
coagulated lumps: buttermilk.
Into this mahogany vessel
I agitate stories into poems
make food from both
the bitter and the sweet.

Crystal Clear

I could see if it wasn't for my thirst for sugar,
how I could set myself free
from the wreck of my pancreas
and its irrational habit of circulating the blood's fire
to blur my stance. It's on me, I know, to get clean.
Some blame mother's milk, where the tooth learns longing,
but, my ache flashes akashic red, black & green
Motherland need or the bitter void of it.

I tried kicking this crutch, but
I always fall below the Mason Dixon line,
I always come up short, empty or high on somebody's story
about my story, plots that don't hold ground.
I want some truth to tide me over
not crystal sweets that don't tend
to this deep hurt I keep trying to feed.

Sugar House

The one that delivers the hit soon forgets.
The one that takes the hit never forgets.
—Haitian Proverb

Ain't nothin sweet in this house.
Blood seeps out of every crevice

the welcome is: chain shackle, metal drag
and whip crack that molests the air.

The Mission? To break black hides—
tear them apart by welt and wound.

This is business—somebody's family tree
carved from each plank board,

prayed on, raised up with Godly intention
with screams soaked into the grain.

Under this roof the Yoke of Goree
is clenched. The collar and Iron Helmet

complete with mouth gag
that squelches the swallow's song,

The iron rings add weight
to clamp the limbs from flight.

The stocks restrict the neck
while the coiled rope break it.

The cast iron pot is thick with boiling
tar. To top it off there's feathering.

Somebody's mind thought this up.
How this house stands for suffering,

to crush what remains of weary flesh
choke the spirit's pilot flame. Somebody

blueprinted this into action—ways to wield evil.
Sugar House a place were misery lives

to add insult to injury. Call it something sweet
that leaves both body and soul for ruin.

Blue Bottles

See them limbs out yonder?
They can bear the brunt.

Branch the blue bottles there.
Better to house a demon in glass.

Siphon hate. Draw the haints.
Never anoint their stir with worry.

'Cause they walk this world
to and fro like tired don't exist.

Better to offer trouble a place to dwell,
Because everything is drawn to the light

'specially evil.

Stomach Trouble

We were never meant to survive
—Audre Lorde

Congenital defect means
my first breath was snatched
by trouble's hand.

It held me before I felt
my mama's embrace.

All five of her babies,
born before time:
I was a whole month shy,

a small mahogany fist of cries
straining against a world
I was not ready to enter.

At 4 lbs. 6 oz.,
I arrived with loss
at my center: umbilical hernia.

My insides
pushing out:
the disposition of a poet.

The doctor waited
four years hoping
the hole would close

It refused.
The disposition
of a poet.

They tied my middle
into a not-so-perfect
in-y knot. I am twisted

by the turns: Duedenum,
Jejunum Ileum, Cecum.
Acid Reflux burn.

My body quakes
from undigested dreams
that I've tried to swallow.

I speak in tongues
with a bitter
aftertaste. I dance

to the involuntary rhythms
of my ancestor's leftover lives.
I stomach trouble, so

I ache and flail
with spasmodic fits
of tongue, pen, and dance.

I rumble
to this burn trying
to turn the chyme.

To the table I came
ill-equipped to handle
what gets stuck in my gut.

Push

move forward by using force to pass people or cause them to move aside

My Father's Ways

Daddy was all things fried—
fish, chicken and pork rinds.
He was also what I'd never been,
pickled pig feet, chitlins
and marrow sucked deep from chicken bones.

On soft days, he was a whole liter of Orange Nehi.
On hard days: three packs of Schlitz Malt Liquor,
when Black Label went out of business,
hot roasted peanuts bought roadside,
a soft pack of Winstons every day,
chased by peppermint or Listerine
to dull the smoke. Lathered
in Old Spice from forehead to big toe.

Then, off around the corner
to the old country store,
The Hub where he ran off by mouth
bragged about us children behind our backs.
Those backs he never saw fit to pat.
I counted Dad's ways as strange.
How he cooked barbecue well done.
Past well done, burnt.

Fight's On

Before daddy developed
a taste for blood,
I wondered if he ever

dreamed of peace
blooming
on his tongue.

The world being
what it is
handed him ends:

He adjusted his taste for salt,
the thump and bump
of high blood.

Pig feet and chitlins,
rearing
into fist.

Our house, his ring—
how he loved
to swing.

We just fell against the ropes
always coming back
to the center

pulled by love
or some deep need
to belong or be touched by him

if only by words
or by fist.
We found our groove,

the bob and weave,
the eggshell dance,
we did upon

his fickle mood.
Forced moves
he taught

my headstrong brothers
to always hear,
fight's on.

This is how he saw fit
to equip them, not with love
but with gloves,

to connect with fist
in the middle of the chest
or an upper cut to the jaw.

This is how they grew to men:
their hard boy bodies
cured like leather,

never resting in time or space,
only to embrace when fatigued.
Hug only to break a fall.

I wonder what daddy
would have become, if raised
on fresh sprouts and fruits,

the sweet juice of life
not the scrawny ends.
Would he still scrap for a fight?

Better fight than cry
Better jab than run
Better swing than die

As the stroke placed
the final blow:
stripped his speech.

His last act,
he forced his fingers.
into a peace sign

as if the world
had finally offered
him a worthy round.

Over the Color Line

It is strange how the stories
move down the family tunnel
with mouths barely open.
How lore still wormed its way,
buried itself deep into our pockets
like unspent coins.
I carry the load. One especially,
how some of Daddy's people gave him grief for
courting Mama with her dark skin and fly away hair
three hues over the paper bag test.
Married her anyway.
That's how I got here
in all my dark presence shining like Mama.

I always thought well of Daddy,
and the ground he took. Until
my brother brought a *yellow gal*
with so-called *good hair* home.
Father congratulated him: *you gotcha a good one, son.*
Was father crossing toward me or was it away?
We were so far apart.
Never heard an "I love you."
Or, "you're pretty." I carry the weight
of what my father never said to me.

South Carolina Love: It's Complicated

Blood and root wind their way around
Piedmont back roads. The veins love
the land, the familiar curves, the sweeping lush
green and the secret fish ponds.

My Palmetto State sells both homegrown peaches
and hate roadside. Every time I try to fit
my mouth around a Carolina Allegiance,
I cannot own the stance outright.

I fly my southern flag sideways.
Riding down Hwy 25 to home,
I am still chilled by the past,
stunted by the sky-size crossbar banners
draping the air with heritage.

Others bathe in homespun love,
I feel shadow and ghost,
with only a little light escaping
through the leaves of the lynching trees.
I'd love to sample only the sweet.

Flagging: What the Confederate Flag Means to Me

(Found poem from Merriam-Webster)

Flag: a piece of cloth with distinctive marks
      to warn or signal to stop
      to send or communicate a message
      to mark, to make or leave a mark on

Verb: to decline in vigor or strength, to become weak or tired
      to hang down, become limp

Outlaws in Fountain Inn, South Carolina

We broke the law, with the words: I do.
not just the ones written on SC law books,

but those codes held deep in the marrow. We stepped
into places many are taught not to cross.

People felt a strong need to voice
their beliefs to me about marrying

across color lines,
any chance they got:

What about the children? As if they cared
about my future offspring. In 1987 my vows

were not a revolutionary stance
just a stubborn bloom reaching

toward what my heart knew to be right.

Ritual

My grief drives me to the barbershop.
Tells Tony to cut my shoulder-length hair

to the quick. He hesitates until
he catches what lingers in my eyes.

Six black barbers click into place,
form a circle of silence around me.

Whitney Houston's voice graces
the moment from the speakers overhead,

For every win someone must fail...
there comes a time when you must exhale.

The last brown tuft drifts to the floor
as the song ends. The men standing

like warriors break rank. Tony takes off
the cape and I step out into the harsh light

of day with my head bare as a bulb.
Grief drives me home.

Two days later in the doctor's office,
I come across a *National Geographic.*

The article speaks to me. It says:
The Masai shave their heads in mourning.

I bend mine, shorn,
let grief in.

For the first time—
I cry for my lost child.

Tilted Bowl

There's no circle
that can bear this load,
not the moon of my mama's face,

or the circumference of his arms
that were supposed to fit around me for life.
In this loss I am alone.

I circle in this flat place
with no wind to wipe away
what loss has made of me.

People try to comfort me
with clichés,
well-meant mumblings

that run through me
hot and useless
as a waterfall gone wrong.

I see my child everyday,
as a brilliant unhinged star
of water, sinew & blood,

sewer-bound floating
underneath the house
where he was meant to grow,

all the days of his childhood.
If I were of a different make,
I would will my mind to forget,

but I live this nightmare even
in the day, a meadow where guilt
flowers on every stem.

I am a woman, a tilted bowl.
I live in this field
where I pick and pluck trying
to bear this spill that I cannot hold.

Muscle Tear

(Anahata)

1.
The condition of my heart
is the wreck you made.
The love songs
have it all wrong.
The heart does not break,
like any muscles
it tears, when you
go against the grain—
rips and bleeds.

2.
Wrap it in ice.
Treat immediate pain.
Rest. Massage and stroke.
Slowly gain muscle strength.
Gently exercise the affected limb.
Build trust. Learn how to love again.

Close as I Get to Cursing

Where I come from, hate seethes
like a fresh brew on the tongue everyday.

Why add to the pot? Bile leaves
an unpleasant aftertaste.

Why lend words to curse the earth?
Aren't our skies full enough of soil-weep

and southern tree-lean? Gut rot grows
in the bowels. I say shit it out.

If ever I hurled a stone, it was in my mind.
Damning the damned ain't worth the spit.

College Education

Baptist Church
Honea Path, South Carolina, 1985

Dear Dean,

> *Please ask your black students*
> *not to return to our congregation.*
> *They are troublemakers*
> *breaking up our church by attending.*

> This letter drizzled
> with Please & Thank You.

Finished off with:
Sincerely Yours,
Signed in Christian love.
by the Minister-in-Charge

God's Will?

The missionaries
God's chosen people to uproot the root;
pave it over on a pure-driven position
to mount the world, save the heathen from
They know not that they know not.
They come pounding a leather-bound belief,
thrust and heave into those below,
just enter the land and ban the drum,
driving hard and high until spent.
Leave. Don't note the—ravage,
the damage. Say, *It's God's will.*
Repeat this mantra.
Assume the position: on top.
Thrust deep and hard.
Do it again, again and again.
Never look into their eyes.

Swimming Lessons

It was the ease
of his dark body sliding
into an unbelievably blue pool

undoing the don't in me,
unbinding middle passage knots
causing them to sing their release—

I watched him glide.

I'd learn this was his language, ease.
Strokes and silver words
unhampered by land-lock fear.

He became my first. The first
black man I had ever seen
navigate water without pause.

It is not like I wanted
to make him more than what he was
in his Trinidadian swagger,
his nonchalant calypso grace:
pulsed my awe

flexed my horizon,
stretched my arc
into an eager fluency
of water,
of words.

The Marsh

Black campers are asked to leave the Valley Swim Club
Philadelphia, 2009

It was in the 80s, the day felt like a swamp
full with the muck of it.
There are some days that hold you thick,
so intense you think, I'll never forget this.

But here I am now wondering
what wing I was in. Was it B or C?
Was I on my way to Algebra II or lunch,
when I caught word that the invitation
had been pulled back for the pool party?

Not jerked from us all,
just the black cheerleaders.
The family didn't want their water tainted.
The words punched like a full-on jab.

How does a 15-year-old brace the heart?
The first instinct is to strike
out like a cobra,
fill the air with righteous rain.

I can't remember now, but somehow
I found my school spirit by Friday,
pumped all the pep I had into the rally,
but the blue and white had begun to fade.

That swimming pool memory
is not so crisp but the swamp
always creeps back into my mind.
I just wanted what all kids want
in the heat of July,
turquoise-blue waters
unwavering and floating
holding me firm above the fray.

We Not That Carefree

Daughters of mine: you are given grief
because you do not camp easily.
You rest hard on open ground
and wrestle with water when you swim.
Remember this: you are my best
of both earth & sky. Do not apologize
for why you don't dig nature, all the time.
You don't have to answer
for the code unleashed
in your bones. You did not cause
the unnatural tilt of trees
or the reflections of a boy named
Emmet Till: cherubic caramel face,
held wide-eyed underwater.

You do not have to jump off cliffs
and simulate Mountain Dew ads
to hold God's green hand.

We have seen
that all around history's ground
is sinking sand.

Benediction

We took back roads cutting cross-country
traveling from one small road to another
snaking from Moonville to Mauldin.
My big brother Willie and I rode
while the blue Duster began stuttering a dubious rattle,
sputtering to a stop on a small rural track of road called Conastee,
a quarter-mile stretch riddled with seven steeples,
each pointing a path to God:
First Baptist, Church of God, Deliverance of God,
United Methodist, Reedy River Presbyterian,
Conastee Fellowship Hall and McBee United Methodist.
Surely we were cloaked in the protection of the Lord
as we knocked on the first door we saw,
a sweet grandma-looking lady
opening her door like a smile
granting us a Samaritan's Act
by letting us use her phone.
Her words spilling over us like gospel,
we heed even today.
Hurry, night's about to fall. You two
are not safe around here.

Chair

For George Junius Stinney, Jr.
Columbia, SC, 1944

At fourteen you sit in a too-big chair,
your feet dangle like a child's. Your five-foot
90 lbs. strapped to a fire that will fry your flesh,
knock the life from your bones. You sit with the word guilty
stamped on your too-small head by an all white jury.
Alone you sit in front of those who sneer
as you sip your last breath. In that chair
their eyes burn into you with their blind truth.
Your family gone; run out of town,
because you told two white girls
where to find Maypops. George Junius Stinney, Jr.
show me the flower of your small hands.
Did they fit around a railroad spike
poised in the air to crush two skulls?
'Cause all I see is a little boy's eyes in search for somebody
—anybody who can hold you in these last minutes,
but you are held only by your own sweat.

I Wish You Black Sons

after Lucille Clifton

For people who believe # Black Lives Don't Matter

I wish you the ability to bear only black fruit
I wish you only sons
I wish them black
spilled from your loins like black ink
I wish you code words like: inner city   urban   hip-hop
I wish you Baltimore, D.C., Newark, Philly, Ferguson and so on...
I wish your sons long walks home
through white neighbors' yards
I wish the neighbors' curtains peak open
I wish they call the cops
I wish you that you live your life on the lip of this terror
I wish you dreaming of ways to whisper protection
in your sons' ears
I wish you the knowledge that these words
won't keep your son safe no matter how you tell him
to be clean cut and respectful and to say: *yes sir and no ma'am*
I wish him natty locs and a grill
I wish him dreaming of revolution
I wish him on the frontline of the fight
tatted up and dressed in black leather
I wish you a minimum wage job
I wish you always a dollar short
I wish you no private or charter school
to keep your child away from bad influences
I wish you a job scrubbing toilets, but your mind always
on your son's trek home as he is tracked like a suspect
I wish you a teenage boy full of shenanigans
I wish that he smokes weed
I wish he gets in fights with his friends
I wish him a boy like any other boy not perfect,
but labeled a thug for life
I wish him stalked by a trigger-happy cop
unloading justified bullets in his black behind,
because he had it coming anyway

I wish that police officer off scott free
time off with pay,
when he kills your son
I wish that police officer $500,000
from his Crowd Funding account
I wish you your son's autopsy report
I wish it shows your son's broken spine
and crushed vertebrae by his own hands
I wish you wondering how he killed himself
I wish you hear in your sleep eleven times: *I can't breath*
I wish you black
I wish you black sons
I wish you dressed in black
I wish you a black mother's worries
and a black father's prayers
I wish you no bandages for your bloodied son
I wish you only tears to wash his wounds
I wish you salt in your wounds:
I wish you Fox News on repeat
I wish you invitations to funerals every week
I wish you a world that cannot see your son,
but for the color of his skin
and not all the shades of how you know your son
from goofy to socially awkward
to wanna be the coolest on the block
wanting to go to prom
wanting a tight haircut and fresh kicks
I wish you not one flower at his funeral
just quotes about black-on-black crime
I wish you a world that never talks
about white-on-white crime
I wish you a stone for a pillow
I wish you awake all night alive in this place
where we have always lived:
1600s   1700s   1800s   1900s   2015

I wish you America
and your black sons are named:
Tamir, Trayvon, Michael, Oscar, Walter, Freddie, and Emmett...
I wish you awake enough to see: black
for what we always have been: black
and what we will always be: black
I wish you sight to take in: black
I wish you both eyes and heart to see
why we don't parade the banner: *all lives matter*
because we know the statistics they don't.
I wish you: us
or at least the ability to see us: black,
but nevertheless like you:
flawed, beautiful and human

Blackbird Reckoning

I am thinking of all of God's creatures
especially the oriole
and how beautiful this blackbird can be
and how its black body should have
a safe place to dwell in both sun & rain.

Today I am thinking of Baltimore,
how it is a song of bullets and sirens
on repeat across the world.
In the trenches of every inner city that I teach.
I see no white, but only black and brown faces.
White flight be borders: private schools
and charter schools draw lines between us & them.

The geography of my heart tells me
Things are not going to get easier,
because Baltimore is: Newark, Trenton,
Greenville, Chicago, Charlotte, Atlanta,
Bed Stuy, Brooklyn, Bronx,
Philly, LA and so and so on . . .

Soon and very soon
the revolution is coming
to a street near you

Today, I am thinking about the Oriole
Blackbird with black tipped wings
brushed with orange: Flight & flame

Pull

an act of taking hold of something and exerting force to draw it toward one

I Misses You

Even in death we can't escape:
       you in dis ragged patch
       passed off as a so-called grave;
       me a steal away at night
       'cause I ain't daylight free.
Gots to come when de land don't call
       between washin clothes
       and wringin chicken necks.
       Sunday be dat day
       no plow touch de ground.
I get here then, but Lawd knows
       your memory calls on me everyday.
       Reminds me how I know myself
       From my name coming out your mouth
       freedom and home in one breath.
I was a well-held cup in your hands
       I won't feel dat whole again
       When your fingers danced on my skin
       I grieves you all de time,
       but I don't let a drop of dis river
       spill from my eye
I tamp down what wails.
       I 21 nails and pine box myself shut.
       I come to dis place where you buried
       to mark my misery—
       no tombstone no name etched—just me
From de earth we came and to it we shall return,
       bible says—I guess it be a blessing—for you,
       I prays you at rest
       on de other side of Jordan,
       but I can't sing *Hallelujah Anyhow*
Dis be de heaviest work I ever done
       carrying on
       carrying you
       living inside my chest

Baseball & Brilliance

For Cornell Foggie, Jr.

You are baseball and brilliance.
We bragged about both behind your back.
How at nine you read the *New York Times*
on the regular. We boasted about
your off-the-chart I.Q.
and how your skills on the diamond
burned with an unmatched fire.

You were our throwback
with Jackie Robinson bearings.
Something about your skin: mahogany deep,
set against your star-white teeth.
and how your tree-like strength
made a stand and took the heat.

I never asked you if # 42 was your hero
and I regret that I never told you
that you were mine.
Even as a boy, I believed you
to be what a man should be: upright and clear.

Rumor was: you were so bright,
that you skipped three grades.
Even your teachers could not keep up
with how your mind ran circles
around your public school classrooms.

You were my polite New York kin
untouched by tenement stench
and the city's exhaust. How did you
out run the bullets of Bed Stuy?

I am sure that you were no saint.
What boy really is?
But, how you inhabited human
made me believe in myself more.
We called you Junior,

but you were senior amongst
most people,
a rare untouchable beauty,

but cancer is thief. Stole your breath.
Took you too soon in your 33rd year.
Yes, my grief is still hot and it took me
fifteen years to pen this loss.
Ironically, you were finishing law school,
but where is the justice in this?

Even now on the street
once in awhile,
I'll see a tree trunk-like man
with the kindest of faces
and I will think of you.

Flashback to your bat hitting the ball—
see the wide expanse of your back
muscles rippling and stretching
in Ogun-like proportions.
I feel the power of your swing
and your stride moving—
like you did in life
running and rounding the bases,
glancing back
for just a moment,
so we can see the flash
of your brilliant eyes and teeth.
Then, your aura vibrant
halo-like heading
to greener grasses
outfield and out of sight,
but not turning
to where we all want you:
home.

Marked by Fire

When I was four I was marked by fire.
I was claimed by the iron's heat—
face, neck and arms nothing but singed skin.
I stank with the aroma of burned flesh.

Possessed by heat I was dunked
under the faucet, slathered with butter,
dashed to a mystic of the South
across a red clay road to someone's house
who knew someone, a woman,
who could *talk the fire out.*
She said my name and spoke in tongues
and then the pain lifted like a quiet wind.

My right shoulder still bears
the brand of an arrowhead
pointing to my heart
as if to say *No wind or tongue
can douse this fire.*

My First Poetry Teacher

For Carrie McCray

Teach like the congregation
at Bethlehem Baptist Church yells *Preach*
and she did. Said, *Poets look back.*
Mine the memory.
Find the journey worth taking.
Don't dismiss the coal.
Go down the dark shaft.
Go down into the danger.
Go down into the lives lost.
Plummet. Clear the smoke.
Wipe your eyes and the grime.
Write.
Polish the rock
that made the past
till all facets
come to light
shine

Bruised

For Middlesex County Academy in New Brunswick, NJ – Alternative School
and Damon House – Alcohol & Drug Treatment Facility

They banter back and forth like boys do:
You charcoal, son. You so black you purple.
I tell them, *hol'up* in defense of my mahogany skin
and the boy they're putting down. I say,
You know what they say? In cue as if we rehearsed it,
we both chime, the darker the berry, the sweeter the juice.
We flash twin smiles. There's a moment when the air
gets less complicated in the room. The space is large enough
for me to ask, *why y'all hate on each other so hard?*

Oh, he? He my boy. See, that's how we show love.
They crush so hard I want to weep—
I'm so tired of everybody being gangsta hard,
but they are being real. I know 'cause I got three brothers
and growin up I never saw them show love,
except in that one on one—man on man dunk in yo face.
Call you *ignant* ten times a day kind of way.
Their talk swags like their walk.
I follow the conversation as it dips and drags.
We end up talking about how we were punished as kids.

I lead with, *I'm from the South and ya'll don't know*
nothin about a switch—havin to go'round back
fetch your own hickory, the same stick use to beat you.
I say these words and I still feel the sting of the switch.
See welts raising into an angry language of graffiti on my skin.
One says, *don't bring back no skinny one neither.*
I shake my head in solidarity—the blood we've spilled makes us kin.
Another boys says, *what about those belts?*
I hear my mama's beating cadence,
a belt whip with every word, *I–told–you–not–to...*

Another says, *extension cord.*
I'm brought fully awake, 'cause
I don't know nothing 'bout that kind of whippin.
We only heard of Cedric down the street gettin beat like that.
Then, we did not know the word, *Abuse,*
or the phrase *Child Protective Services.*
We just said his mama was MEAN.

Jicante, another says, I say huh? *Rice.*
You kneel on raw rice for hours.
We walk down alleys; I listen as they go deeper
into the shadows farther than I have ever been,
but we don't skip a beat.   We laugh—
joke about our beatings and nobody mentions
the pain, but it's all understood—we are all battered.
We bump up against each other's wounds before we brainstorm.
I pick up the marker and they bicker blue versus red.
I read between the gang signs. It is not lost on me,
that when these colors mingle, they make purple.
I muse in my mind how violence for them still continues.
I come back to the poem, that we are here to write;
the ones that saved my life. I know this detour we took
down old roads is a place we had to go,
places where we have been loved so hard it hurts,
so hard we are still bruised.
We bear our scars,
then we pick up our pens
and write.

The Tao of the Black Plastic Comb

Bless my bad ideas and butt whippings:
the black plastic combs passed out on picture day.
Bless my taking the comb and listening
to the blond haired girl promising: *I can make you pretty.*
Bless me for wanting to be pretty,
but obviously lost in the whitest of seas
floating on a Kindergarten raft with no sign of help
via a mirror or a black girlfriend to keep me from going astray.
Bless my Ramona the Pest ways, always getting it wrong—
collar and ribbon upturned always at the other end of mama's,
dag nam your time' chile.
Bless the five years that I had already spent on this earth
those years already filled with my school girl sense of shame
wearing Pigpen's dusty aura like a shadow that I could not shake.
Bless mama's tug of war with each strand.
Bless my *tender headedness* that matched my heart.
Tender. Nothing, but tender—too tender
for my mama's heavy hands
that did not know their own strength,
pulling each strand on my head through the hot comb,
during this Saturday morning ritual.
Bless her command: *don't let nobody touch your hair.*
Bless my ears not hearing.
Bless the brewing of sorrow and regret that are already in my eyes.
Bless the back of the camel broken by the straw.
Bless my backside the day the pictures arrived home,
when my mama saw my hair as what she called,
something the cat drug in.
Bless my eyes and the load they were already carrying.
Bless me a high-strung girl feeling like my families' punch line,
when they saw my first school photo each laugh felt like a jolt.
Bless how I learned to pocket the hurt in my heart.
Bless this act of survival.
Bless the small tines of the black comb: The teeth. The bite
that every hand is not a helping one.
Bless the little white girl who did not see my beauty.

Bless me for not seeing my beauty—
the years it took for me to unlearn self-loathing
and not one hair on my head that needed touching.
Bless this little girl within me waiting
to come back to this picture with a smile,
seeing myself as cute and lovable
with sandalwood smooth skin and the deepest amber eyes
scrying already like a poet.
Bless my little girl-self waiting for my return
to make the connection between then
and now: my hair now loc'd and woven,
wrapping myself with both forgiveness and release.

Apologia to My Double Ds

I.

While other girls' breasts trained in bras,
mine came here full "C" cupped
not as girls, but as grown-ass women.
At nine, too young to carry the gift
grandma and her mama handed to me
I felt only burden, not yet the power
that these backbone women toted.
Their breasts turned abled tongue men
into stutterers and stammerers.
Great-grandma wet-nursed her sixteen
and almost the whole town of Waterloo.
How my foremothers boasted
of their busts without shame.

II.

I was in their club, but I had to disappear
to walk down catcall high school hallways.
I locked and loaded you
into sensible blazers to block gazes.
The jeers made me feel violated
like I was showcasing stripper tits.
Mama's voice weighed heavy too,
their the first thangs people see when you walk into a room.
I could not yet utter the word *beautiful.*

III.

My breasts, forgive me
when I could no longer carry you.
Had you trimmed to ease my back burden,
But you came back proud with the last laugh
like Grandma Katie
like Great-Grandma Rachel
taking a stand.

IV.

You ewers of homegrown milk,
you fed my twin babies,
your headrests haven for lovers and children.
I see now as I carried you,
you carried me.
Forgive me my journey,
the long way 'round
into my own ample inheritance.

We Swag before Doorags

I am from if you have to ask *never mind.*
If you don't come from no way cut into way,

you'd just waste my time by asking why.
There's not enough meat hanging on metaphors

for me to explain how my back got built
—not taken from slick pages, but fashioned

from a tenuous foundation of make do.
I am from before doorags—stockings

cut, tied and worn to bed, Murray-made waves.
Father made them. Rode his rage right out

of Jim Crow's South—his bones set
in Muddy Waters and Howling Wolf Blues.

Wind and water: Hate-spit that beat
and battered the spirit. Daddy played

by ear what he could not say.
I come from—it'll learn you,

if you'll listen to how music mixes
fear and pride. Between the notes

sorrow calls out—drops of bitter blood,
Mama always made it better. Sugar:

white or brown. Stirred by hand.
Our veins burned. Her table always set

with grace and love. Bible verses circled.
My brothers prayed short cuts, *Jesus wept.*

We did too. Laugher holds the tears,
fever swells and swollen limbs.

I am from Spades: cards of strife.
Getting cut. Going in the hole.

Renig. We talk much smack,
as we climb out of our past dug.

We step on the family ladder
rung after rickety blessed rung.

Danced before we could walk,
We stand upright, but rooted

to pocket poor, but spirit rich,
a life that taught how to tie—stretch.

Make a dollar from fifteen cents.
Common sense—we had plenty,

schooled us in bend but not break,
our eyes closed. Our hands tied

around our lack. Curved around
hambone hambone where you been?

Hungry. We made songs to feed
Our dreams deferred with words,

to keep us from exploding.
Our teeth clenched with *everyday*

*something has tried to kill me
and has failed*. We vow to free.

We spin the edict of slave. No. *We were never meant to survive.*

We thrive. *We real cool.*
We make do. We twist this.

We flip the mask from scowl
to mirth. We do what we do:

Squeeze blacker berries to make
sweeter juice. Our walk not a dirge,

but dance. Each step. We do swag.

28 Day plus All the Rest

What can I say about a month? February—
28 days is not enough.
I will take those days and raise you 337 more

—a lifetime bet. Bet den.
Bet these stories intentionally buried,
that I dig for like medicine,

most of them bitter:
Tongue and drum taken.
I beat and speak on my own accord.

I'm drinking in as much healing
as I know how.
This sound I sing: American History.

There was no blues/jazz/spiritual in the math
they tried to teach me,
how I figured less and less

I had to find the root,
the truth
I had to squeeze the juice: I'm more.

I carry the root to schools,
let the students catch hold. I pour
what my Ogun grandma taught me: you more.

Her 3rd grade schooling taught her
Iron words that she walked:
I don't have do nothing but stay black and die
and that's what she did after 109 years.

She stayed true. Me too.
Like my grandma sang:
I'mma stay black
I'mma stay on the battlefield till i die.

Cotton & Cane

Fire on my tongue & calico touchin skin makes me lay back.
Love sugar on my lips & soft on my sway back.

Mama say cotton ain't that soft—cane ain't that sweet neither.
Pulls stories from her cross-wise sack, tells how she kept prey back.

Walkin down white-hot rows carrying 350 pounds
makes a body bend & holler, What you say, back?

Cotton & sugar stirs the ache. Mama ain't nobody's
fool waitin on 40 acres & a mule payback.

Cotton pierces dreams & cane hacks the soul. Lives come
up short, when cotton is the only light bringin day back.

Love soft tufts & sweet drinks, but mama's words
kick dirt, boil blood conjurin red in the clay back.

South rounds our mouths, Africa do too,
'cause we spit words like *ofay* back.

Knowin gnaws & haunts me like a haint. Got bottles
on tree limbs in my bones and the blues on playback.

Love juiced up fire and field cotton blooms hi-jackin
me, bringin ol' songs like *Steal Away* back.

Old folks' songs sung off-key pierce the veils,
throw me to the past, I don't sashay back.

Gotta love you, Glenis, you crook-neck black Sankofa,
Can't unkink this hold—you an old soul from way back.

Genealogy

Mus tek cyear a de root fa heal de tree.
— Gullah proverb

I can only beget
so much—wrestling

with limb break
and early leaf fall.

So I bend my body
in both work

& prayer. Pull
& dig stories up

by the root.
Plunk them down,

water & turn
green verse

walking between
the worlds.

All Is Possible

For Julian Josiah

Julian Josiah, you make me grand,
the only royal title I'll ever own

> You, a treasure:
> 10 fingers: starlit
> 10 toes: eager squiggles

Your cheeks: squishy pockets
earned you the nickname: the chipmunk gnome.
Your eyes: lit with the deepest shine, déjà vu remembrance.
Your 9 lbs. 3 oz., substantial weight
you'll carry what's been passed on:
the walk of the ancestors.

This legacy is also a burden
I know your legs will be sturdy
and worthy of the task
like Yusef Komunyakaa writes:

You were born
to wear out at least
one hundred angels.

Like Maya Angelou penned
You come as one but stand as ten thousand
you will carry this load with wisdom
and undeterred stride.

Julian, all is possible with you.
Unflinchingly I will sing
of the more I want to give you
what John Lennon dreamed
imagine there're no countries
it isn't hard to do
nothing to kill or die for.

Julian, I am a dreamer; it is all that I have:
the gift of my imagination.
You are surrounded by
the perfect O of love.
Family willing to grow you
from black boy to black man
to walk into this world better
than the one I/we are handing to you,
like Langston Hughes wrote,
I hope you'll dream a world
where love will bless the earth,
because you are part of that blessing
lighting the world with the brilliance
of what you came to do.

Notes

It is estimated that during the slave trade at least 10 million Africans, and perhaps as many as 20 million were brought to American shores.

After the Middle Passage, over 40% of the African slaves reaching the British colonies before the American Revolution entered in through the port city of Charleston, South Carolina.

In the United States, interracial marriage, cohabitation and sex have since 1863 been termed "miscegenation." South Carolina passed six miscegenation statutes in 1865. Though they were overturned in 1967, South Carolina did not remove its prohibitive clause from their law books until 1998.

Black Codes 1.9–29
If any slave shall teach, or attempt to teach, any other slave to read or write, the use of figures excepted, he or she may be carried before any justice of the peace, and on conviction thereof, shall be sentenced to receive thirty-nine lashes on his or her bare back. *(1830 c 6 s 2)*.

Although the last recorded lynching in South Carolina—that of Willie Earle—It took place in 1947. Earle, a black man, was being detained in Greenville, South Carolina, having been accused of the stabbing and robbery of a white cabdriver. Twenty-six white men dragged Willie Earle from jail and took him to Saluda Dam near Bramlett Road. Though he professed innocence, he was silenced with a shot to the head. All twenty-six men were found not guilty; no blacks were allowed to serve on the jury. The ramifications of this unjust history still echo in South Carolina and throughout the South. In "Nature Lesson" I conflate Willie Earle's lynching with the many that came before, often in the form of hangings. As a child, when my mama told me the story, I always imagined him hanging from a tree.

Footnotes

Where does history go
when it hasn't been tended?
I say it grows wild amongst the Periwinkle,
the Turkey-foot fern and my mind.
There it is right alongside my heart.
Heavy like that mass of stones left on a hill.
The only remnants left of the Kingdom
speaking of mountain royalty,
King Robert and Queen Louella
leased for ten cents a day
by a Civil War widow named Serpta.
Their rule was over 200 acres
of chopping, hauling and toting.
I understand this urgency,
the need for self-appointment.

I hear voices on the ridge
I hear them crying out on the wind
about the uneasy quilt-stitch hearsay
of their lives being left to myth and lore.
Where does history go when it dies?
Where does it go, when corn cribs
and makeshift houses no longer
riddle the mountain slopes
when forty years of hands
culling Comfrey into a balm
comes to an end,
where gospel songs cease?
This silent edge is where I live
where history goes without a foothold,
heartache filled with remembering—

A Note from the Author

To my most immediate family: Celeste, Amber, Julian and Jeanette, you all inspire me to do and be my best. You all are my September Birth People, my sapphire touchstones. We are all Virgos. You help me to stay grounded.

A special thanks to my mama, Jeanette Redmond: you taught me about craft by first demonstrating mastery, while sewing and cooking for our family. Your love, patience and wisdom have helped me to stay focused and encouraged.

To my Cave Canem family, thank you for the much-needed fellowship and a place to develop my craft.

Many thanks to my Peace Center family, especially to CEO, Megan Riegel, and Vice-President of Education, Staci Dillard Koonce, by creating a space for poetry in the Greenville, South Carolina, community.

Many thanks to the State Theatre in helping me to create a second poetic home in New Brunswick, New Jersey. Lian Farrer, thank you for your leadership at the helm, and to Erik Stratton for being a constant support mode with a smile on your face.

Thank you to the Kennedy Center for the Performing Arts' Barbara Shepherd and Amy Dumas for believing in the work that I do as a poet and teaching artist.

Because I am Bi-Carolinian I would like to thank the arts councils in two states. The South Carolina Arts Commission and the North Carolina Arts Council and the Metropolitan Arts Council. Thank you for your support via grants to help me develop as a poet and a teaching artist. Thank you also for fostering my twenty-two years as a poet and a teaching artist. Also, much gratitude to EMRYS for your support throughout the years.

Thank you to Kevin Morgan Watson for the final edits and for publishing my third collection, and a major shout out to Kwame Dawes, who believed in this manuscript and, with his editorial eye, helped me to shape *What My Hand Say*.

To this poetic path in particular, thank you, God/Goddess, the Great Spirit, the one who rules the Universe, for having my back and for helping me to stay centered and not losing myself along the way. Thank you for my connection with the ancestors. As Maya Angelou says, *I come as one, but stand as ten thousand.*

To all who have helped me along on my poetic path: I fully understand that it indeed takes a village to raise a poet; therefore, I embrace the African phrase *Ubuntu: Because you are, I am.* For this I hold much gratitude in my heart for the village that has helped to raise me to my present poetic height.

Glenis Redmond travels nationally and internationally reading and teaching poetry so much that she has earned the title, Road Warrior Poet. She has posts as the Poet-in-Residence at The Peace Center for the Performing Arts in Greenville, South Carolina, and at the State Theatre in New Brunswick, New Jersey. During February 2016, at the request of U.S. State Department for their Speaker's Bureau, Glenis traveled to Muscat, Oman, to teach a series of poetry workshops and perform poetry for Black History Month.

In 2014-16, Glenis served as the Mentor Poet for the National Student Poet's Program to prepare students to read at the Library of Congress, the Department of Education, and for First Lady Michelle Obama at The White House. Glenis is a Cave Canem Fellow, a North Carolina Literary Fellowship Recipient, and a Kennedy Center Teaching Artist. She also helped create the first Writer-in-Residence at the Carl Sandburg Home National Historic Site in Flat Rock, North Carolina.

Glenis believes that poetry is a healer, and she can be found in the trenches across the world applying pressure to those in need, one poem at a time.

Visit Glenis at www.glenisredmond.com

Cover artist April Wilson Harrison paints images primarily in acrylics, powders, watercolors, pencils and collage. She finds that working with this unique palette offers faster drying times, enabling her to overlay color in one painting session, giving the work its tapestry-like background. She often incorporates found objects into her paintings, such as coins from around the world, specialty papers, magazine print, and interesting treasures that she finds on the street. Even nearly discarded paintings are given new life and recycled into newer works of art, thus creating texture and dimension.

She is a self taught artist and believes that she is merely a vessel being utilized to instinctively create narrative, sentiment, and observation. She is humbled by this gift.

Her paintings are the result of internal communication that require expressions of acceptance, pride, adoration, and dignity. In creating these images she has come to appreciate artists who have been granted diverse narratives. April believes that when art moves the heart and awakens the spirit, it makes no distinction as to its originator.

Find more of April's work at AprilSongGallery.com

CPSIA information can be obtained at www.ICGtesting.com
Printed in the USA
BVOW08s2013191016

465503BV00001B/4/P